ANATOMY OF A HONEY GIRL

(POEMS FOR TIRED WOMEN)

Anatomy of a Honey girl

(POEMS FOR TIRED WOMEN)

Liz Houchin

SOUTHWORD*editions*

First published in 2021
by Southword Editions
The Munster Literature Centre
Frank O'Connor House, 84 Douglas Street
Cork, Ireland

Set in Adobe Caslon 12pt

ISBN 978-1-905002-91-7

Contents

FIGURE IT OUT
A model, an actress and two pop girls make up our four famous dollies below.
If you admire their looks see how your statistics compare with theirs
when you fill in all your details in the column to the right.

—*Fabulous 208 Annual, 1969*

The Droste Effect

Mary Quant retrospective at the V&A, July 2019

There is a temple on the Cromwell Road
a place of worship to the gods of cool, to seek
absolution from shapeless high street sins.

I bowed and blessed myself with matcha tea
rummaging for lip gloss, imposter without poise
wanting to blend or no, wait, wanting to hide

among the curated daisies and Twigs on show
under lights releasing the musk of Youth Dew
wafting over minis and Sassoon bobs bobbing

out of plastic macs over long-legged boots.
And then the music in my head stopped dead
faced with an unholy celebration of underwear:

booby traps promising *your own sweet self*
(minus six pounds)' and the anatomy of a girl
who reads *Honey* magazine and understands

dieting to disappear
inside the recursive
image of ourselves
getting smaller
getting smaller
getting smaller
all the time
always.

Camo, 1978 (wool)

An army green jumper knitted in four squares for my brother's Action Man who literally lost his shirt in a parachute accident off the flat roof.

Wedding Flowers, 1980 (cotton)

A string of crocheted daisies cut from my mother's wedding dress and sewn on my communion dress to make it— and by extension me—less plain.

Cat's Eye, 1981 (polyester)

Carrying bag for marbles made from old brown curtains. According to my marble champion brother it was as strong as a saddlebag.

Gold, 1981 (satin, rope)

A red satin cloak for my Nativity debut as Melchior, tied around my neck with a length of rope which until that point was securing a drape.

Rabbit, 1988 (wool, plastic, thread)

A collaboration with my younger sister who forgot to finish or even start her knitting project, complete with odd button eyes and a wry smile.

Now You See It, 1985 (300 thread count cotton)

One of her finest achievements. A self-proclaimed invisible mending of a Woodbine cigarette burn in my grandmother's quilt from America.

I

place your thumb under her chin
stretch your index to her chest
measure her neck in licks

move your thumb lower now
inch your way round her cage
decide what dress will fit

stand her up tall and straight
lift your boot against the wall
tell her how she grows

lead her to the garden remove
your belt and lay it flat
let her know her yard

that's the measure of a man.

II

the men at Cornell
burned her palm
during labour
to create
the unit
of pain
what
a dol

ERASURE

what is it about (me)
you are so afraid of?

every time I dare / think
I am drawn in permanent marker

you take something   away

and I realise to you I am
only an idea sketched in soft 2B
/vulnerable to your fingertips

I rub my eyes (gently) and try
to understand your endgame:

do you want   me to not be?
do you want   to be me?

you smell victory either way
but really, have you thought this through?

as you sharpen your pencil
to imagine me again
getting smaller all the time
(but point well made)

you will only have yourself to blame

rough twine between my lips
an old bird holding a dead worm
gingerly tying in floppy shoots
clematis and sweet pea

ink on my tongue
a venomous invitation
coaxing a pen back to life
for just one more line

a damp parking ticket
between traffic-clenched teeth
the only safe place in my car
searching for the exit

sand on a lollipop
dropped by a sunburnt child
smiling as I return it before
spitting and swearing inside

these are the only things
I wish to put in my mouth
that are not food.

WATCHING A FRIEND BECOME AIRBORNE

you knew your flying weight
trained and sweated and starved
for your title fight with the stars

understood the translucency
necessary for the wind to take you,
onion skin aerogram by gram

I denied the beauty of you
as a gowned pane backlit by the sun
rising, catching the wheeled pole

that tethered your larking kite,
a fraying line slipping through
the fingers of a wingless world.

ISLAND PICNIC FIGHT

Silence has a scent, he said, like the sea but not the hot
orange boiled sweet sucked shiny week in Spain sea

no, not that sea, the other one—tumbling growls
spraying cold gusts of grey foamy old woman spittle

I could not speak above the attrition, rounding us
like pebbles fit for palms before eroding us to sand

That May we were on Saltee and we began on song
our song stuck on repeat scratch happy happy hap hap

ha-ha then nothing but the pressured pop of needled love
leaving only the summer gale blowing through the crevice

prised open between bodies in retreat, standing on the beach
wrapped in layers taped shut by bumped and braided arms

We turned our backs to the bluebells and waited to ferry
home the dregs of us and our basket of crusts and cores

On second thoughts

Now that you're here, would you chop me down
  —cleave me open—show me what I'm made of?
I wonder if my insides (split and polished as you do)
swirl like burr walnut flares of copper, caramel and coffee.

Or maybe my insides are Scandi cool select-grade limed
oak in a timeless herringbone pattern quietly reflecting
the clear white light of beauty, truth and innocence.

Or perhaps it would be best if neither you nor I chance
knowing what makes me. Leave me as I am, rooted in place
fully barked against human wilt and accept occasional offerings
of blossom and fruit as evidence of what lies beneath.

CAST OFF

When we cast on, years ago, knitting our love sweater
we followed our own pattern, starting with a slipknot
new needles click clacking as we found our rhythm
uneven at first, our threads pulled a little tight in places
—but too fine a gauge to worry about strangulation—
we counted stitches in twos, like heartbeats, watching
lines of plain settle smooth into our unthinking centre

a u t o m a t e d l o v e l i v e s
m a c h i n e d m o n o t o n y
p e r f e c t p a r a l l e l p a i r

But there it was: a peephole, there, in line seventeen.
Who was counting after all this time? Me, I never stopped.
I wonder if you had already noticed the dropped stitch,
untethered, a loose loop ready to unravel us all the way
and perhaps you let it drop to allow some other's light
illuminate your exit while I fumbled with a crochet hook
to ladder us back up again, to make us look like new.

Anni

Anni Albers exhibition at Tate Modern, November 2018

She sits sepia still
a cantilevered frame
in the Bauhaus way

bentwood arms down
           swept / rest on her loom
              scrolled hands hold the weft

calico headscarf
frames her maple face
belies her gilded past

ribbed vase back drawn
           forward by the threads
              interrogating life tapestryclose

feeling my way
—like a horse in fire—
fingertips following her haptic trail

cotton and rayon cresting and falling
           a bedform of sand
              rippled by yarn obeying the grid

a twist in the road now
redacted plateau
blind only to the eye
      revealing your truth to my thumb
            to the end still under your threaded trance
            knotting temple cyphers / beauty in the flecks

INTERCESSION I

for Anni

he came from Thebes, stopping in San Moritz
picking up the thread that led to me

still in his armour he removed his helmet
black curls fell and framed his Egyptian face

I rushed to tidy, shuffled papers into piles
bunched pens, sank coffee cups in the sink

sorry about the mess—I don't know where to start
you already have, he said, all you needed was a thread

INTERCESSION II

for Anne

In times of rubble
and demolition
catch your breath
while the dust falls

Tie back your hair
lace up your boots
cover heavy ground
as lightly as possible

Start with fragments
the sound of a car horn
the zip on a dress
the last word she said

Her head full of words
the words that she said
now words in your head

Rehearsal

I imagine you passed and consider the curve
would the ascent—your ascension—defeat me
or would I summit grief only to tumble down
and land not on my feet, as you would?

We will wake you, you and I, over tea and cake
and I will tell you everything that I would tell
a heaving chapel or command a choir to sing
your praise and plead you not to leave.

To the opera student in room G-17

Sposa son disprezzata

I can't see you but imagine
thick black hair fierce blue eyes
spritzed with tears as your teacher
stops your song again and again
demanding more and more

higher
longer

send him out to the corridor
where I sit on a blue plastic chair
waiting the music mother's wait
as my child tames a wild piano
scaling grades pedalling tunes

adagio
andante

all I can hear are angels.

THE CAREGIVER

Leaving her house
alone she met
a young wren
flat on the path
onyx eye
pert beak
splayed wing
arranged
as if for pressing
between sheets
of blotting paper
a feathered bloom
for winter pleasure
she was so grateful
it could not be saved

A DRIVEWAY MOMENT

I sat in my car and danced
turned up the radio
turtle bobbed my head
from side to side
joined in with the chorus
N-n-n-no, no, no, no place I'd rather be

BEAUTY AND THE BEECH

I knew what they were saying
behind handfuls of confetti
under hatfuls of flowers
      'there she goes marrying a tree'

silly girl and her silent knight
taciturn and towering over
callow pea green saplings
      'in a sludge brown suit in June!'

who dared speak as one vow
cartwheeled down the aisle
one murmured on the breeze
      'I'd say he's some barrel of laughs'

the band played and I twirled
gazing at my spotting point
as they raised a mocking glass
      'let's toast beauty and the beech!'

    but the day gave way to crickets and stars
        my dress lay puddled on the forest floor
           and my ear pressed to his rippled trunk
               heard sparklers and peonies and pearls.

MELLIFIED WOMAN

'For honesty coupled to beauty, is to have honey a sauce to sugar.'

Shakespeare, *As You Like It*

I

Where is all this going? So much vanilla and rose
lavender and grapefruit souring on my skin
smeared and sprayed blurring and masking.

You wait for me to understand—your patience stretched
over seas and centuries like the skin of an animal
bred with teeth and tongue for honour and respect.

I'm a Standing Girl to sand and polish
cloths and creams sloughing my grit revealing
my grain to the light from the torch you carry.

The beauty supernova is just an infinite star chart
of fool's sparkles and shiny rewards shooting towards
a black hole I can't see—where is all this going?

II

The A to my Q came not from vintage *Vogue*
but an ancient myth of mellified monks, my fate
my script engraved in your familiar hand

(you wrote other myths too, presented as lists
because I am slow witted, 101 ways 50 ways 3 ways
to satisfy to shine to fill the space you shaped for me)

The monks—there's always a monk—did not believe
in diets and creams, booby traps and dyes and chose
honey—there's always honey—for their sacrifice

ate honey, bathed in honey until death by honey
buried in a casket filled with honey for a hundred years
transfigured into a healing human confection.

III

Human confection. Sweet! How sweet that I have practised
being sweet all my life, palatable and moreish to your gaze.
It makes sense now. Finally, you say, your role is clear

as clear as honey with the pollen filtered out, no sediment
of me to spoil the dream of Ménerbes in summer, the blurring
beauty of Kate's highlights, Cindy's shins, you spooned me

you can watch me. Keep a diary and write another list/myth
'the Honey girl guide to human confection,' rhyme it
with perfection and smile from the whitened teeth out

helpful hints for when it sticks to your hair clags in your throat
how to be happy when you cry honey bleed honey sweat
honey when your breasts leak honey, it's all for you, honey.

IV

It won't be long now. You have been waiting for me, standing
outside the bathroom door where jars filled with clover
orange blossom and acacia emptied down my throat

to slake your thirst for girls and dolls crowd every surface
like midnight on New Year's Eve. I close my eyes lower
my amber body as lobes of honey lava advance on my flanks.

You guided me here. A drone over a lifelong unicursal
labyrinth of makeovers and mirrors—a climax of illusion
that the path was mine and joined with yours by chance.

You will still be here in a hundred years, ready to serve me
on a spoon dipped in a casket of medicinal sweet—melted
to a poultice for your scars, healing what is wrong with you

consume me and call me Mellona.

FIGURE IT OUT

Model	Singer	Actress	Actress
18 years	21 years	25 years	19 years
6 ½ stone	8 stone	10 stone 8lb	7 stone 10lb
size 8	size 10	size 12	size 8
twice a week	twice a week	twice a week	twice a week
orange juice	cup of tea	alouette	Dubonnet
Leonard	Leonard	Paul	Ricci at Vidal
Mousey / Blue	Dark Brown / Blue	Gold / Blue	Red / Blue
thigh 16 ½"	thigh 18"	no idea	thigh 19"
ankle 8 ½"	ankle 7"	no idea	ankle 6"

Acknowledgements

Heartfelt thanks to the Creative Writing faculty at University College Dublin, especially Jonathan C. Creasy, Julie Morrissy and Paul Perry.

For sharing their wisdom and time, thanks are due to Richard Price and Jade Cuttle at The Poetry School and Sasha Dugdale, Carrie Etter, Fiona Sampson, Mark Doty and Caroline Bird at Arvon.

Special thanks to Scott, Benjamin, Harriet and Toby for their love and inspiration and to my mother and father for instilling their love of reading and writing.

To Felicity and Estelle, my long-suffering first readers, thank you both for your friendship, encouragement and good humour.

Sincere thanks to the Arts Council of Ireland for supporting my work.

"the measure of a woman" first appeared in *Banshee*.